F1
NU
Activity Book

Fran Newman-D'Amico

DOVER PUBLICATIONS, INC.
Mineola, New York

Welcome to the world of number fun! You will add and subtract, count different types of animals, color by number, connect the dots, find the largest or smallest, look at shapes, and even learn how to tell time. Along the way you will see cute pictures of farm and circus animals and other things that can be counted or compared.

If you need help with an answer, look at the Solutions section, which begins on page 51. Don't peek until you've tried your hardest. For even more fun, color in the pictures with colored pencils, crayons, or markers. Let's get started!

Copyright

Copyright © 2006, 2020 by Dover Publications, Inc.
All rights reserved.

Bibliographical Note

Fun with Numbers Activity Book, first published by Dover Publications, Inc., in 2020, is a republication in a new format of *My First Book of Number Fun*, originally published by Dover in 2006.

International Standard Book Number

ISBN-13: 978-0-486-84467-1
ISBN-10: 0-486-84467-6

Manufactured in the United States by LSC Communications
84467601
www.doverpublications.com
2 4 6 8 10 9 7 5 3 1
2020

How Many Do You See?

	1
	2
	3
	4
	5

Count the birds in each row.
Trace and write the number on the lines.

Bug Hunt

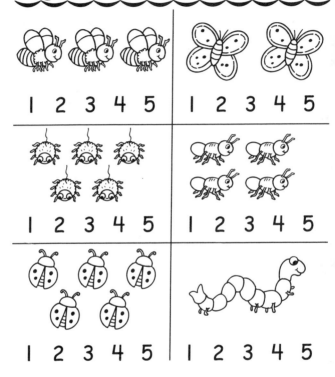

1 2 3 4 5

1 2 3 4 5

1 2 3 4 5

1 2 3 4 5

1 2 3 4 5

1 2 3 4 5

Count the bugs in each group.
Circle the number that tells how many.

More to Count!

🍎🍎🍎🍎🍎🍎	6 _ _ _ _ _ _ _ _ _ _ _ _ _ _
🍌🍌🍌🍌🍌🍌🍌	7 _ _ _ _ _ _ _ _ _ _ _ _ _ _
🍐🍐🍐🍐🍐🍐🍐🍐	8 _ _ _ _ _ _ _ _ _ _ _ _ _ _
🍓🍓🍓🍓🍓🍓🍓🍓🍓	9 _ _ _ _ _ _ _ _ _ _ _ _ _ _
🍒🍒🍒🍒🍒🍒🍒🍒🍒🍒	10 _ _ _ _ _ _ _ _ _ _ _ _ _

Count the fruit in each row.
Trace and write the number on the lines.

Circus Friends

$$\begin{array}{r} 3 \\ + 2 \\ \hline 5 \end{array}$$

$$\begin{array}{r} 1 \\ + 1 \\ \hline \end{array}$$

$$\begin{array}{r} 2 \\ + 2 \\ \hline \end{array}$$

$$\begin{array}{r} 1 \\ + 3 \\ \hline \end{array}$$

$$\begin{array}{r} 4 \\ + 1 \\ \hline \end{array}$$

Count the things in each group.
Write the number.

Busy Barnyard

A Day at the Beach

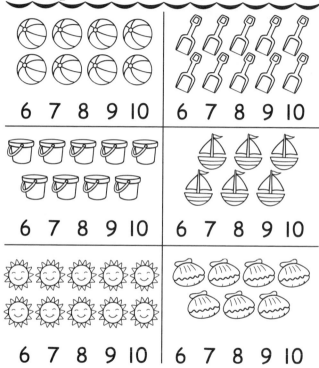

6 7 8 9 10   6 7 8 9 10

6 7 8 9 10   6 7 8 9 10

6 7 8 9 10   6 7 8 9 10

Count the things in each group.
Circle the number that tells how many.

Seaside Friends

1	2	3	4	5
one	two	three	four	five

1

2

3

4

5

Fun with Sports

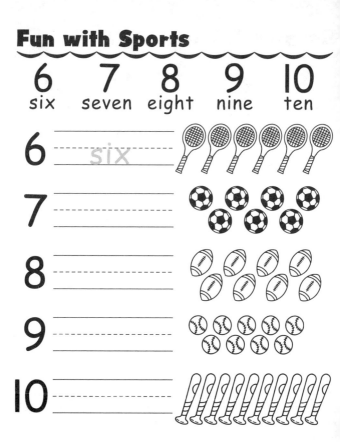

6 six   7 seven   8 eight   9 nine   10 ten

6 — six
7 —
8 —
9 —
10 —

Write the number word for each group.

Fish Fun

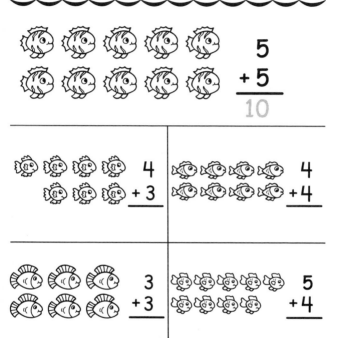

$$\begin{array}{r} 5 \\ + 5 \\ \hline 10 \end{array}$$

$$\begin{array}{r} 4 \\ + 3 \\ \hline \end{array}$$

$$\begin{array}{r} 4 \\ + 4 \\ \hline \end{array}$$

$$\begin{array}{r} 3 \\ + 3 \\ \hline \end{array}$$

$$\begin{array}{r} 5 \\ + 4 \\ \hline \end{array}$$

9

Coloring Fun

Color this picture of a hungry giraffe.
1 = red, 2 = light blue, 3 = yellow,
4 = brown, 5 = dark green, 6 = light green

Bunny Hop!

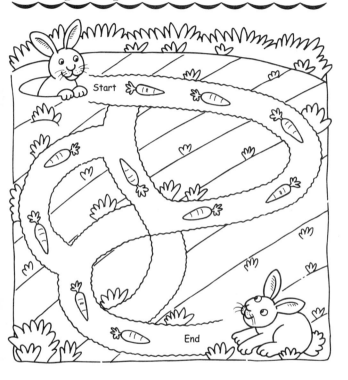

Draw a line through the carrots to help the bunny
find his friend. Count the number of carrots you
find along the way and write it here: _____.

What Am I?

Connect the dots from 1 to 10 to
see a picture of this creature.

Playtime

Which group has more? Color it yellow.

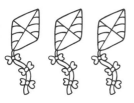 

Which group has more? Color it red.

Which group has more? Color it blue.

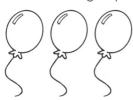 

Count!

Color the cake with the most candles.

Color the friend with fewer balloons.

Color the flowerpot with the most flowers.

Top, Middle, Bottom

Color the birds on the TOP of the fence red.
Color the birds in the MIDDLE of the fence yellow.
Color the birds on the BOTTOM of the fence blue.

Follow the Leader

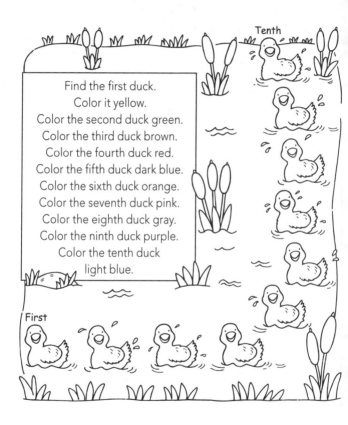

Find the first duck.
Color it yellow.
Color the second duck green.
Color the third duck brown.
Color the fourth duck red.
Color the fifth duck dark blue.
Color the sixth duck orange.
Color the seventh duck pink.
Color the eighth duck gray.
Color the ninth duck purple.
Color the tenth duck
light blue.

Tenth

First

Largest and Smallest

The largest one is circled.

The smallest one is circled.

Circle the largest.

Circle the smallest.

Circle the smallest.

Circle the largest.

First, Next, Last?

Each row tells a story. The first row is done for you. For the second and third rows, tell what happened first [1], next [2], and last [3]. Write the numbers in the boxes.

Different

In each row, circle the animal that is
different from the others.

Match

Draw a line from each baby animal on
the left to its parent on the right.

Shapes, Shapes, Shapes

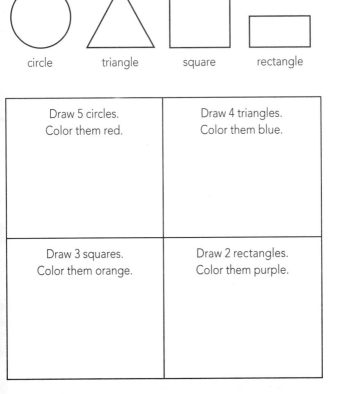

circle   triangle   square   rectangle

Draw 5 circles. Color them red.	Draw 4 triangles. Color them blue.
Draw 3 squares. Color them orange.	Draw 2 rectangles. Color them purple.

Circus Shapes

Count the number of each shape in the circus picture and write it on the line. Remember to count a shape even if it is turned upside down!

Shape Patterns

Look at the shapes in each row.
Draw the 2 shapes that come next.

Pattern Fun

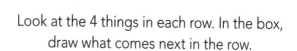

Look at the 4 things in each row. In the box,
draw what comes next in the row.

Purr-fect Fun

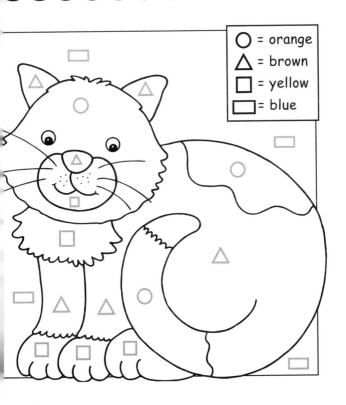

○ = orange
△ = brown
□ = yellow
▭ = blue

Use the shape code to color the picture.

Garden Friends

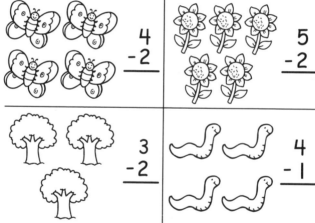

$$\begin{array}{r} 5 \\ -1 \\ \hline 4 \end{array}$$

$$\begin{array}{r} 4 \\ -2 \\ \hline \end{array}$$

$$\begin{array}{r} 5 \\ -2 \\ \hline \end{array}$$

$$\begin{array}{r} 3 \\ -2 \\ \hline \end{array}$$

$$\begin{array}{r} 4 \\ -1 \\ \hline \end{array}$$

Subtract. Put an X on the things you took away.
Write how many are left.

Sky Search

10-5 = _____

8-6 = _____

7-4 = _____

9-2 = _____

Subtract. Put an X on the things you took away.
Write how many are left.

Flying Frenzy

4 ⬜ 1 = ‗‗‗

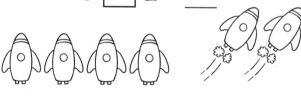

1 ⬜ 4 = ‗‗‗

6 ⬜ 2 = ‗‗‗

Add or subtract to find the answers to the math problems
Write a plus or minus sign for each problem.

28

Mousematics!

Add or subtract to find the answers
to the math problems.

Calendar Quiz

Sunday	Monday	Tuesday	Wednesday	Thursday	Friday	Saturday
1	2	3	4	5	6	7
8	9	10	11	12	13	14
15	16	17	18	19	20	21
22	23	24	25	26	27	28
29	30					

June

What month is this? _____

How many days are in one week? _____

How many days are in this month? _____

How many Sundays are in this month? _____

How many Tuesdays are in this month? _____

Birthday Wishes

What is your birthday month? _____

In the space above, draw a picture
of your favorite birthday gift.

Two by Two

Trace the numbers as you count the socks by twos.

2 4 6 8 10 12 14 16 18 20 in a

Count the number of mittens by twos. Write the numbers.

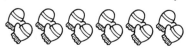

__ __ __ __ __ __ __ in all.

Count the number of buttons by twos. Write the numbers.

__ __ __ __ __ __ __ __ __ in all.

Count the number of shoes by twos. Write the numbers.

__ __ __ __ in all.

Count from 11 to 15

Count the things in each row.
Trace and write the number.

Count from 16 to 20

🎁🎁🎁🎁🎁🎁 🎁🎁🎁🎁🎁 🎁🎁🎁🎁🎁	16 --------------------
🧁🧁🧁🧁🧁🧁 🧁🧁🧁🧁🧁 🧁🧁🧁🧁🧁	17 --------------------
🎈🎈🎈🎈🎈🎈 🎈🎈🎈🎈🎈 🎈🎈🎈🎈🎈	18 --------------------
🎉🎉🎉🎉🎉🎉 🎉🎉🎉🎉🎉🎉 🎉🎉🎉🎉🎉🎉🎉	19 --------------------
✏️✏️✏️✏️✏️✏️✏️ ✏️✏️✏️✏️✏️✏️✏️ ✏️✏️✏️✏️✏️✏️	20 --------------------

Count the things in each row.
Trace and write the number.

34

High Fives!

5	10	15	
25		35	40
45	50		60
65		75	80
85	90		100

Counting by fives, write the missing numbers in the boxes. Start at 5 and end at 100!

Who Am I?

Connect the dots from 1 to 25 to
see a picture of this flying animal.

Learning to Tell Time

Color the clock face yellow. Color the hour hand green. Color the minute hand red. Color the numbers blue. Color the rest any way you like!

What Time Is It?

The hour hand is on 3.
The minute hand is on 12.
It is 3 o'clock (3:00).

5 o'clock 8 o'clock	9 o'clock 3 o'clock
10 o'clock 7 o'clock	6 o'clock 2 o'clock

Circle the correct time for each clock.

Half-Hour Time

The hour hand is
between 4 and 5.
The minute hand is on 6.
The time is four-thirty (4:30).

2:30   8:30

9:30   6:30

10:30   7:30

3:30   4:30

Circle the correct time for each clock.

Time Test

What time do you get up?
Draw the time on the clock.

What time do you eat lunch?
Draw the time on the clock.

What time do you go to sleep?
Draw the time on the clock.

Inches

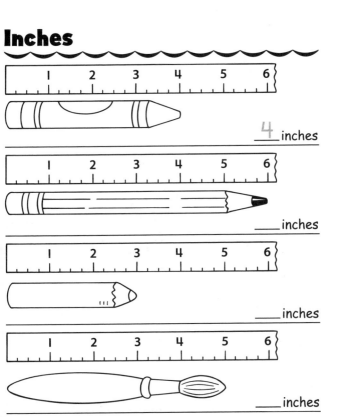

	1	2	3	4	5	6	

_4_ inches

____ inches

____ inches

____ inches

Use each ruler to measure the thing below it.
Write the number of inches.

Centimeters

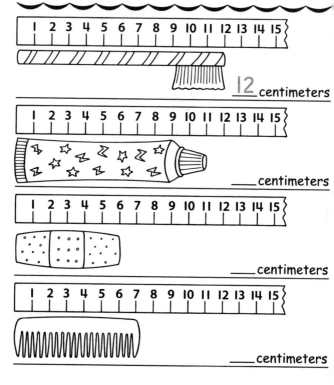

1 2 3 4 5 6 7 8 9 10 11 12 13 14 15

_12_ centimeters

1 2 3 4 5 6 7 8 9 10 11 12 13 14 15

____ centimeters

1 2 3 4 5 6 7 8 9 10 11 12 13 14 15

____ centimeters

1 2 3 4 5 6 7 8 9 10 11 12 13 14 15

____ centimeters

Use each centimeter ruler
to measure the thing below it.
Write the number of centimeters.

Pennies, Nickels

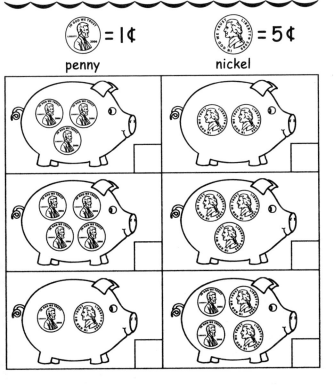

= 1¢

penny

= 5¢

nickel

Add up the coins in each piggy bank.
Write the amount in the box.

Dimes, Quarters

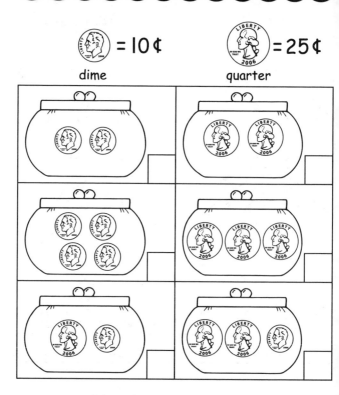

= 10¢

dime

= 25¢

quarter

Add up the coins in each purse.

Write the amount in the box.

Money Math

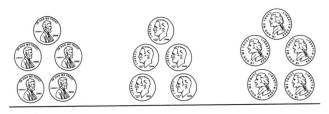

Add up the coins in the groups in each row. Circle
the group in each row that has
the greatest amount.

Coin Match

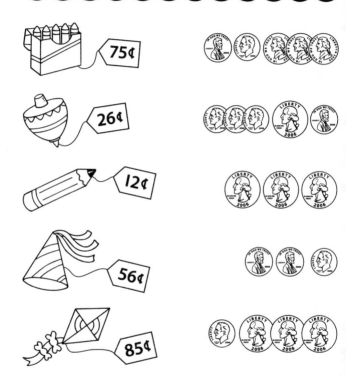

75¢

26¢

12¢

56¢

85¢

Draw a line from each item to the group
of coins you would need to buy it.

One Half

This circle has two parts that are
equal (the same size).
Each part is one half.
Two halves together
make one whole.

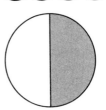

Circle the shapes that are made of two halves.

 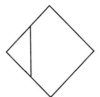

Draw a line in each shape to make two halves.

Half Practice

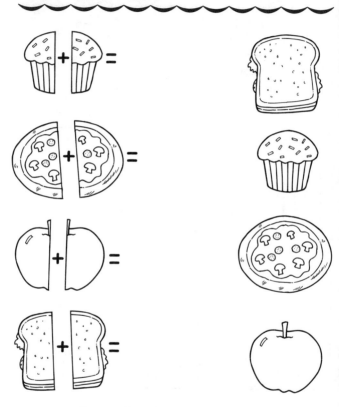

Draw a line from two halves to
the whole that it makes.

One Fourth

This square has four parts
that are equal.
Each part is one quarter.
Four quarters together
make one whole.

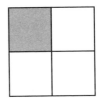

Circle the shapes that are made of four quarters.

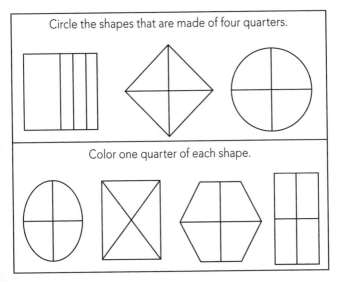

Color one quarter of each shape.

One Third

This circle has three parts that
are equal.
Each part is one third.
Three thirds together
make one whole.

Circle the shapes that are made of three thirds.

Color one third of each shape.

Solutions

Bug Hunt

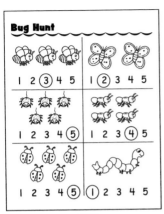

1 2 ③ 4 5   1 ② 3 4 5

1 2 3 4 ⑤   1 2 3 ④ 5

1 2 3 4 ⑤   ① 2 3 4 5

page 2

Circus Friends

$$\begin{array}{r} 3 \\ +\ 2 \\ \hline 5 \end{array}$$

$$\begin{array}{r} 1 \\ +\ 1 \\ \hline 2 \end{array}\qquad \begin{array}{r} 2 \\ +\ 2 \\ \hline 4 \end{array}$$

$$\begin{array}{r} 1 \\ +\ 3 \\ \hline 4 \end{array}\qquad \begin{array}{r} 4 \\ +\ 1 \\ \hline 5 \end{array}$$

page 4

Busy Barnyard

page 5

A Day at the Beach

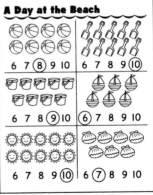

6 7 ⑧ 9 10   6 7 8 9 ⑩

6 7 8 ⑨ 10   ⑥ 7 8 9 10

6 7 8 9 ⑩   6 ⑦ 8 9 10

page 6

51

Seaside Friends

1 one	2 two	3 three	4 four	5 five

1   one

2   two

3   three

4   four

5   five

page 7

Fun with Sports

6 six	7 seven	8 eight	9 nine	10 ten

6   six

7   seven

8   eight

9   nine

10   ten

page 8

Fish Fun

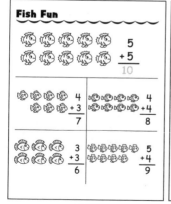

$$\begin{array}{r} 5 \\ +5 \\ \hline 10 \end{array}$$

$$\begin{array}{r} 4 \\ +3 \\ \hline 7 \end{array} \qquad \begin{array}{r} 4 \\ +4 \\ \hline 8 \end{array}$$

$$\begin{array}{r} 3 \\ +3 \\ \hline 6 \end{array} \qquad \begin{array}{r} 5 \\ +4 \\ \hline 9 \end{array}$$

page 9

Bunny Hop!

Start

End

10 carrots

page 11

52

What Am I?

page 12

Playtime

page 13

Count!

page 14

Largest and Smallest

page 17

53

First, Next, Last?

page 18

Different

page 19

Match

page 20

Circus Shapes

◯ 3   ▢ 3   △ 7   ▭ 9

page 22

54

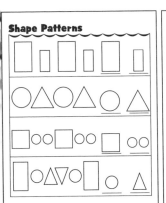

Shape Patterns

page 23

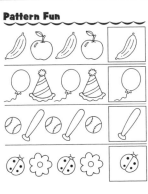

Pattern Fun

page 24

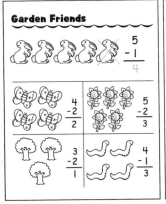

Garden Friends

$$\begin{array}{r} 5 \\ -1 \\ \hline 4 \end{array}$$

$$\begin{array}{r} 4 \\ -2 \\ \hline 2 \end{array}$$

$$\begin{array}{r} 5 \\ -2 \\ \hline 3 \end{array}$$

$$\begin{array}{r} 3 \\ -2 \\ \hline 1 \end{array}$$

$$\begin{array}{r} 4 \\ -1 \\ \hline 3 \end{array}$$

page 26

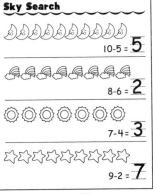

Sky Search

$10-5 = 5$

$8-6 = 2$

$7-4 = 3$

$9-2 = 7$

page 27

Flying Frenzy

$4 - 1 = 3$

$1 + 4 = 5$

$6 - 2 = 4$

page 28

Mousematics!

$$\begin{array}{c}5\\+4\\\hline 9\end{array}$$

$$\begin{array}{c}-10\\5\\\hline 5\end{array}$$

$$\begin{array}{c}3\\+3\\\hline 6\end{array}$$

$$\begin{array}{c}-9\\1\\\hline 1\end{array}$$

$$\begin{array}{c}4\\+1\\\hline 5\end{array}$$

$$\begin{array}{c}-6\\2\\\hline 4\end{array}$$

$$\begin{array}{c}-7\\2\\\hline 5\end{array}$$

$$\begin{array}{c}4\\+4\\\hline 8\end{array}$$

$$\begin{array}{c}+1\\\hline 2\end{array}$$

$$\begin{array}{c}2\\+2\\\hline 4\end{array}$$

$$\begin{array}{c}-9\\3\\\hline 6\end{array}$$

$$\begin{array}{c}5\\-1\\\hline 4\end{array}$$

$$\begin{array}{c}-7\\2\\\hline 9\end{array}$$

$$\begin{array}{c}-10\\5\\\hline 5\end{array}$$

$9 + 1 = 10$

$$\begin{array}{c}4\\+3\\\hline 7\end{array}$$

page 29

Calendar Quiz

°❀°June°❀°

Sunday	Monday	Tuesday	Wednesday	Thursday	Friday	Saturday
1	2	3	4	5	6	7
8	9	10	11	12	13	14
15	16	17	18	19	20	21
22	23	24	25	26	27	28
29	30					

What month is this? ___June___
How many days are in one week? ___7___
How many days are in this month? ___30___
How many Sundays are in this month? ___5___
How many Tuesdays are in this month? ___4___

page 30

Two by Two

_2_ _4_ _6_ _8_ _10_ _12_ _14_ _16_ _18_ _20_ in all.

_2_ _4_ _6_ _8_ _10_ _12_ in all.

_2_ _4_ _6_ _8_ _10_ _12_ _14_ _16_ _18_ in all.

_2_ _4_ _6_ _8_ in all.

page 32

56

High Fives!

5	10	15	20
25	30	35	40
45	50	55	60
65	70	75	80
85	90	95	100

page 35

Who Am I?

page 36

What Time Is It?

page 38

page 39

page 40

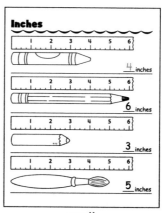

page 41

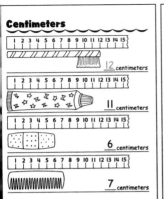

Centimeters

1 2 3 4 5 6 7 8 9 10 11 12 13 14 15

__12__ centimeters

1 2 3 4 5 6 7 8 9 10 11 12 13 14 15

__11__ centimeters

1 2 3 4 5 6 7 8 9 10 11 12 13 14 15

__6__ centimeters

1 2 3 4 5 6 7 8 9 10 11 12 13 14 15

__7__ centimeters

page 42

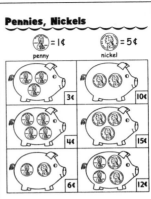

Pennies, Nickels

= 1¢
penny

= 5¢
nickel

3¢

10¢

4¢

15¢

6¢

12¢

page 43

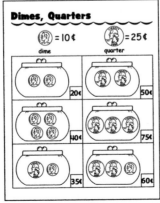

Dimes, Quarters

= 10¢
dime

= 25¢
quarter

20¢

50¢

40¢

75¢

35¢

60¢

page 44

59

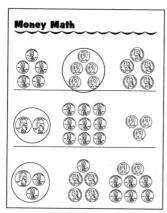

page 45

page 46

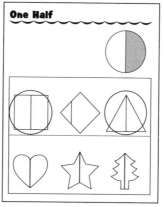

page 47

60

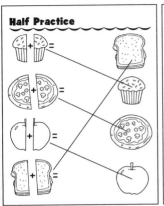

page 48

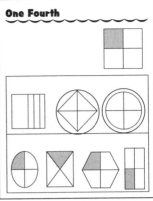

page 49

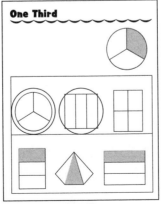

page 50

61